COLLECTE

Other books by James Michie

Poetry
Possible Laughter
New & Selected Poems

Translations
The Odes of Horace
The Poems of Catullus
The Epigrams of Martial (selected)
La Fontaine: Selected Fables
Euripides: Helen
Aesop's Fables (selected)
Poems from the Greek Anthology (selected)
Ovid: The Art of Love

COLLECTED POEMS

JAMES MICHIE

SINCLAIR-STEVENSON

First published in Great Britain in 1994
by Sinclair-Stevenson
an imprint of Reed Consumer Books Ltd
Michelin House, 81 Fulham Road, London SW3 6RB
and Auckland, Melbourne, Singapore and Toronto

ISBN: 1 85619 316 0

A CIP catalogue record for this book
is available from the British Library.

Typeset by Rowland Phototypesetting Limited,
Bury St Edmunds, Suffolk

Printed and bound in Great Britain by
Cox & Wyman Ltd, Reading, Berkshire

For Jake, Drogo, Flora and Edward

CONTENTS

ix

Author's Note

The first of these poems to be printed appeared in *Penguin New Writing* in 1950, the last in this year's *Spectator*. I have made no attempt to present them in a chronological or any other kind of arrangement. Some of them have been lightly revised since their first publication.

I hesitated before including the section entitled *Epigrams and Oddities* on the grounds that it might be viewed as a very lightweight job-lot. However, once 'Out of a Hot Lapis Lazuli Sky' had appeared in an anthology, and the pseudonymous 'For Bonny Elspeth' been read at the Edinburgh Festival as if Hamish MacBride existed, and the parody 'The Porter's Vision' been piously reproduced in a London parish magazine, I decided to let history take its course.

J.M.

POSSIBLE
LAUGHTER
1959

Quiet, Child

My cry-baby indignation,
   House is empty. Parents out.
Too late now to raise a protest.
   Nobody can hear the shout
Little angry injured persons
   Utter under history's clout.

Underneath mad hands of barbers,
   Helpless, sheeted like the dead,
Here we sit and watch the lather
   Tinge alarmingly with red,
And wonder if besides the whiskers
   Experts will remove the head.

The impotent like pills, the nervy
   Swallow war like benzedrine;
The mechanically minded
   Get mashed inside their own machine;
Even the Epicurean porker
   Turns a Christian Gadarene.

Finding water will not flow, the
   Gun-shy spirit leaves the eye,
And the tongue within its burrow
   Dies in arsenic of the lie,
And the trunk of being rots, which
   Means and stands as straight as I.

Glumly we chew on with murder
   Long past the appetite of hate.
Nothing but their shadows' outlines
   Left, like grease-stains on a plate,
People leaning over bridges
   Quietly evaporate.

And big as a telephone directory
    His bomber's casualty list,
Gloved, the pilot leaves behind him,
    Represented by a mist,
Individuals who were furious,
    But no longer now exist.

Hush, my infant indignation,
    We must keep quiet, you and I,
Or someone will report our lively
    Howling. Members must be sly
In our small and banned society –
    Those who do not want to die.

For a Friend in the Country

God knows how you find yourself so entertaining!
My hollow places fill with momentary envy
Seeing how one with so many Furies can be
Perpetually refreshed by himself. The same thing

Would drive me mad; for long ago detecting
Nothing, I gave up the search for myself sadly.
The apple, who longed for a stone, accepted a medley
Of pips in the end, a dozen selves, all acting,

And came to terms with its heart. But, like your spring,
You listen to yourself, certain of your identity,
And talk to yourself with no horror of aridity,
Exchanging unambiguous whispering.

Diaries, old letters, long walks and daydreaming,
Addressing oneself or persons imaginary –
The vulture that feeds on others is your kept canary.
Courageous townsmen run away exclaiming

With terror at your pastimes. The cedar waxwing
Perches at evening. You watch it through binoculars
With a horse and dog like the ones on calendars.
God knows how you find the company so relaxing!

The End of the Sage

At the end of his time the sage
Became light like a balloon.
They thought him mad
For dancing and saying hurrah
With the small voice he had.
Queer in a prisoner of that age.

'Much wiser and much dafter,
Now that I quite agree
To become dead,
I achieve a witticism,
And I see at last,' he said,
'Hazy like foothills possible laughter.'

Before the young guard's gun
Could beat sense back into
A head so light,
Fooling his tormentors,
That old man died outright,
Silencing, falling flat like a pun.

The Robin and the Lark

Tail like a painful splinter,
Sham blood running down his chest,
Robin makes the best
Of begging, and with 'Oh sir', 'Please sir' acts
Orphan all winter.

Type of the time-server, he thieves
By a trick of doleful pertinacity
Housemaid's pity,
Picturesque bread and water, but does not see
That the world disbelieves.

And feathers his nest better
Than true outcasts, unheard sufferers,
Since man prefers
To miserable thanks in charity
Cheerfulness from the debtor.

Yet forfeits by the stratagem
The larger adulthood of larks,
Who set up marks
Too high for themselves, and are frozen flying;
Odes are for them,

Death, like a cold comet,
Falling and failure. Robin, at home
With pram wheel, garden gnome,
Is nursery-rhymed, and, limed with children's praise,
Cannot fly from it.

Rhyme Rude to My Pride

O my intolerable
Pride, the rebel
Cain to my Abel,
My life-long trouble,
My hump, my double,
My Siamese growth,
You are destroying us both
By the enormity
Of your deformity.
Have some pity
For both of our sakes!
Look, how your arrogance takes
Us far from friends
Down the long dead-ends
No one defends,
Up cul-de-sacs
To fight (with our backs
To a wall of error
And one eye on the mirror)
The spuriously stoical,
Thick-headedly heroical,
Stiff-neckedly moral
Lost cause of a quarrel
That you've picked with life.
As with a mad wife
Uncontrollable
In the street or at table,
For your sordid
Sake I am avoided.
Even at your best,
Elegantly dressed
In ideals, you're inhuman
Like some fashion woman

Whose silly cult
Of the different and difficult
Is a general insult.
In your noble attitudes
I suspect worse platitudes
Than the ones you escape.
In your monkish shape,
My mesmeric twin,
I see Rasputin
Making my foolish czar
Of a heart unpopular
With the uneducated,
The by now infuriated
Loves and Simplicities.
Worse than all this, it is
You who have stalked away,
Muttering 'cliché',
From morals and money
And matrimony
And each kind ceremony
Of life. Yes, I see
You have tricked me up a tree
To observe mankind,
And now too late I find
That the high-minded
Look blue-behinded
From below, from above
Quaint to the glance of love.
O cacodaimon,
Ingrowing Timon,
Puritanical
Mask, manacle,
Tumour, since no one can
Ever trepan
Us into one man,
And since, if we tried

To commit suicide,
You, my Pride,
Would be too proud and I'd
Be too terrified,
Let us therefore decide
To stand side by side
Without meum or tuum.
For example, this poem
Is hopelessly ours
Along with the stones and the flowers
And the people who throw 'em.

Be a Bear

Shaking a box marked 'Please
Support our organised mess',
The approachers are not given
The opposite of yes,

Except where in dark rooms
The uncharitable live,
Developing their own lights
From a repeated negative.

Right, if you like, as saints,
Blind, if you'd rather, as moles,
When the thunder-clap invites
They shake and head-shake in their holes,

While better-minded beasts,
Too civil to refuse,
Gregariously add
To the weeping and the news.

Lion

Lion with the face of God
Hid in a cloud of hair,
Walking worried and just,
Making of captivity
A fabulous desert of pride.

Heraldic, self-possessed
Lion serious as pain,
Yellow as topaz, erupting
Out of a bleak field
Into our imagination.

Sand-throated lion in the glare,
Swamp lion howling, winter lion
Guarding a sunny pose
Even in the east wind.
Lion dreamt or seen in cloud.

King lion with no people,
Roaring enough to shake
Leaves, if there were, from trees,
Breaking and so making
Silence, portentous, alone.

Park Concert

Astounding the bucolic grass,
The bandsmen sweat in golds and reds
And put their zeal into the brass.
A glorious flustered major heads

Their sort of stationary charge.
Their lips are pursed, their cheeks turn pink;
The instruments are very large
Through which they render Humperdinck.

The sailors and the parlourmaids
Both vote the music jolly good,
But do not worry if it fades
As they stroll deeper in the wood

Where twenty French horns wouldn't stir
A leaf. The intrepid band try not
To mind the applause (as though it were
A testing fusillade of shot),

Polish their mouthpieces and cough,
Then throw their shoulders back to play
A Pomeranian march. They're off!
And Sousa scares the tits away.

Pan

He touched me among
Secluded pines,
Rooted my tongue
And shook my bones.
Like Atlas, my back
Felt the cleansing storms,
Sensations of rivers
Purged my arms,
And with the worms,
Where the dead raise barrows
Struggling to get free,
I ate, and the marrow
Magnified me.
As, meeting in a passage,
Two halt at loss,
Time stood before me
But could not pass.
Not a minim of wind
Lay in the scales.
My eye perceived
The racing snails
Among green pillars,
And marked the stages
Of the falling cone;
From the hills' hid cellars
Sulphurous truths
Burned on the ridges
As I came for the first time
Into my own.
Shedding my ruins
Like a winter snake,
Terrified, laughing
For my new skin's sake,

I felt in my chest
A hardening stone,
Then knew that my enemies
Could nail me down
Twenty times, but I
Would get up again,
Compact and alone,
The unslayable man.

Arizona Nature Myth

Up in the heavenly saloon
Sheriff sun and rustler moon
Gamble, stuck in the sheriff's mouth
The fag end of an afternoon.

There in the bad town of the sky
Sheriff, nervy, wonders why
He's let himself wander so far West
On his own; he looks with a smoky eye

At the rustler opposite turning white,
Lays down a king for Law, sits tight
Bluffing. On it that crooked moon
Plays an ace and shoots for the light.

Spurs, badge and uniform red
(It looks like blood, but he's shamming dead),
Down drops the marshal, and under cover
Crawls out dogwise, ducking his head.

But Law that don't get its man ain't Law.
Next day, faster on the draw,
Sheriff creeping up from the other side
Blazes his way in through the back door.

But moon's not there. He's ridden out on
A galloping phenomenon,
A wonder horse, quick as light.
Moon's left town. Moon's clean gone.

The Nostalgist

His is the house where everything
  Jumps up like a Labrador,
And, trying to greet him, drags him sadly
  And intently to the floor.

A jack of clubs in a dark drawer
  Gives him a fright;
Glass paperweights howling with snow
  Gulp him inside.

Army in perpetual retreat,
  His thoughts going over old ground
Cannot disguise the disgrace by wearing
  Their boots the wrong way round.

From cups and jugs grim little Lars
  Pick at his heart
Like a banjo, or, accordionists,
  Squeeze out old times.

On step and rail the sunbeams slyly
  Hint at somewhere else.
So many things to slip on and tumble
  Down staircases, down years . . .

The worst room contains a bed,
  Love-letters, skates,
Maps with a rosy India, dead
  Fox-trots, and him.

Delos: Alcaics

'According to the Hymn of Homer, the wandering Latona took refuge at Delos, where she gave birth to Apollo. . . . The Emperor Julian, we are told, consulted the oracle, with some degree of affectation, in A.D. 363' (*Blue Guide*).

Men really tried here, harder than ever, but
Again achieved just wildnerness, suicide.
    Reptiles, a failed race too, look up at
        Columns they once could have overshadowed.

Where gods are born, men suffer most, leading or
Led. Here a strong man, oracle-mongering
    En route for those bad lands of Persia,
        Wasted a bit of the breath he lost there.

Heat calmly holds; sea-colour immutable
Also. The flies with sunset to live till, the
    Tourists, their prospects stretching further,
        Hover excitedly round the spots where

Most blood was let out; leaving behind them the
Hairpins and coins whence other intelligence
    (Wave paler, sun less red) will guess at
        Date of disaster and end of effort.

My Woman of the Rich

I did once, more
Than I do now, feel
Jealous of her bridegroom,
And longed for the genteel
Legs and the pretty womb
In that pink-walled and oystery room.

Now I'm glad to get up
From each hard bed
Of my woman of the rich.
To be properly comforted
I run away and stretch
Myself out drunk in a ditch.

Though her body paddles
In the great mild sea,
Her heart thinks it wicked,
So swaddled in virginity
No heatwave could make it
Take off its clothes and dive naked.

On the Death of 2nd Lieutenant Browne

Archetype of all we sensed
We had gone to war against,
Browne and his few wits
Parted, blown to bits.

Though now less lively
Just as unlovely
As when sound of limb,
His men dispose of him,

And, turning snobbish, burn
With shame to have had to learn
Death at the same school
As the lout and the fool.

A History

Above, flowered colossal voices.
I pushed my way through the stalks,
Thankful for being hidden
From God and the bad hawks.

One day the noise bent down,
A savage-looking bloom;
So I put my head in my hands
And lived in that shuttered room

Where the four doors opened
North south east and west
Over sheer drops, and the windows
Shivered when they were undressed.

To celebrate my safety
And to make doubly sure
Of my strength, I made my fists
Bleed on the furniture,

Then descended, afraid of myself,
Moodily outside,
Where owing to my neglect
The giant flowers had died.

Their booming inaudible,
Each face, a withered shred,
Lay limply. I stood
Alive inspecting the dead.

Alone on the scythed plain,
Aghast at solitude, I knelt
Praying for a single tree
On which to hang my guilt.

Then a creature came from nowhere
And took the crimes from my hands
And hung them all over herself
Like necklaces or armbands.

And we shook each other to force
The extremity of love
And raved, but the words rising
Would not marry above.

'I was not looking for you.'
'And I did not want to be found.'
Turning to prefer the desert,
We saw our two wrists were bound.

Nightmare

Panicking alone in chloroform
The child awakening, when the fire is
Weak as a jelly and barely warm,
Calls, but sees in its parent's iris
Equal alarm, and so begins to cry
For solider reassurance than a worried eye.

And finds, since sympathy only shelves
Skeletons into cupboards deeper
And comforters talk to cure themselves,
The waker must walk as alone as the sleeper;
Pains are not charmed by visitors in furs,
Nor devils conjured out by passionate amateurs.

Goodbye

The wrongly married drive off
To applause, for everyone feels
Envy for those taking corners,
Even if on three wheels.

Embarking regiments
In two minds sing,
Glad to go but sorry
To reach the campaigning;

And the dots on the deck, growing smaller,
Feel larger with relief
As the thrill of mere movement
Dissipates mere grief.

O airports, tops of trees,
Ships' sirens, platform bells,
Blonde hair flying beside
Motor-gloved farewells –

Whatever else begins
Some obligation ends.
So, passenger and well-wisher,
Wave cheerfully at bends.

October

And further into
Real death, the bigger blur of space,
But visibly only into the gulf of winter
The city falls –
This capital with a load of dying gardens,
Passengers, monuments, circuses, shining urinals –
Like a paper tossed over a cliff
By a bored reader. Sorrily we wonder if
Autumn is His disappointed face.

The heart feels drowned
As leaves like lifeboats lowered in the air
Capsize in a sea of wind and sink to the ground.
Railway stations
Stand choked with long goodbyes and struggling lovers
Punishing one another with no explanations.
This month it feels good
To go to war, be rabid or misunderstood,
Become graffiti artists in despair.

Quick, draw together,
This time be simple, join hands, sing anything
To counter the rotten whisper in the weather.
That dreary voice,
It seems from a dog-tired oracle, is nothing
But the echo of indecision. Cities, experts in choice,
Engined, unlike the leaf,
Can scale again the weak spirals of grief,
Zoom back to summer on a home-made wing.

I Like You But . . .

I like you but lie to you all, and you never guess.
'There goes', you say, 'one of the frank. Not a bit
Shy of old dishonour or abashed to confess
What others blush to dissemble, he will sit
In the bar with us, his heart on his sleeve.' Yes,
But jackdaws only jar their beaks on it.

What I said to her about love, or she to me,
Is all for your hearing, and my drunk eye waters
With sentiment, for I can afford to be
Confidential, who make you into porters
To take loads off my mind. No secrecy
Is half so safe as publishing three-quarters.

That way nothing is left to be inferred
From my silence, and you reward me for my showing
What costs me nothing. O jackdaw world, poor bird
To know only what I like to think of you knowing,
And to take that nailed-up weathercock, my word,
As a sign of the wind, whichever way it's blowing!

The Deserter

He ran away anywhere, till the dream
That had trailed him waking was lost. A stream
Stumbled and caught itself and ran
Perfectly on. Peace began.

He lay on his coat on top of a hill,
Useless, while he felt his will
Bleed away and in his head
Neutral liquid run instead –

White internal tears of the brain,
Such as, after weeks of pain,
Clear-headed past belief,
Invalids let fall in relief.

Then felt quite happy to be shot,
Knowing, thoughts of escape forgot,
What it was that had made him run away:
Not fear, but a frenzy to disobey.

Dooley is a Traitor

'So then you won't fight?'
'Yes, your Honour,' I said, 'that's right.'
'Now is it that you simply aren't willing,
Or have you a fundamental moral objection to killing?'
Says the judge, blowing his nose
And making his words stand to attention in long rows.
I stand to attention too, but with half a grin
(In my time I've done a good many in).
'No objection at all, sir,' I said.
'There's a deal of the world I'd rather see dead –
Such as Johnny Stubbs or Fred Settle or my last landlord,
      Mr Syme.
Give me a gun and your blessing, your Honour, and I'll be
      killing them all the time.
But my conscience says a clear no
To killing a crowd of gentlemen I don't know.
Why, I'd as soon think of killing a worshipful judge,
High-court, like yourself (against whom, God knows, I've
      got no grudge –
So far), as murder a heap of foreign folk.
If you've got no grudge, you've got no joke
To laugh at after.'
                        Now the words never come flowing
Proper for me till I get the old pipe going.
And just as I was poking
Down baccy, the judge looks up sharp with 'No smoking,
Mr Dooley. We're not fighting this war for fun.
And we want a clearer reason why you refuse to carry a
      gun.
This war is not a personal feud, it's a fight
Against wrong ideas on behalf of the Right.
Mr Dooley, won't you help to destroy evil ideas?'
'Ah, your Honour, here's

The tragedy,' I said. 'I'm not a man of the mind.
I couldn't find it in my heart to be unkind
To an idea. I wouldn't know one if I saw one. I haven't one
   of my own.
So I'd best be leaving other people's alone.'
'Indeed,' he sneers at me, 'this defence is
Curious for someone with convictions in two senses.
A criminal invokes conscience to his aid
To support an individual withdrawal from a communal
   crusade
Sanctioned by God, led by the Church, against a godless,
   churchless nation!'
I asked his Honour for a translation.
'You talk of conscience,' he said. 'What do you know of the
   Christian creed?'
'Nothing, sir, except what I can read.
That's the most you can hope for from us jail-birds.
I just open the Book here and there and look at the words.
And I find when the Lord himself misliked an evil notion
He turned it into a pig and drove it squealing over a cliff
   into the ocean,
And the loony ran away
And lived to think another day.
There was a clean job done and no blood shed!
Everybody happy and forty wicked thoughts drowned
   dead.
A neat and Christian murder. None of your mad slaughter
Throwing away the brains with the blood and the baby
   with the bathwater.
Now I look at the war as a sportsman. It's a matter of
   choosing
The decentest way of losing.
Heads or tails, losers or winners,
We all lose, we're all damned sinners.
And I'd rather be with the poor cold people at the wall
   that's shot

29

Than the bloody guilty devils in the firing-line, in Hell and
    keeping hot.'
'But what right, Dooley, what right,' he cried,
'Have you to say the Lord is on your side?'
'That's a dirty crooked question,' back I roared.
'I said not the Lord was on my side, but I was on the side of
    the Lord.'
Then he was up at me and shouting,
But by and by he calms: 'Now we're not doubting
Your sincerity, Dooley, only your arguments,
Which don't make sense.'
('Hullo,' I thought, 'that's the wrong way round.
I may be skylarking a bit, but my brainpan's sound.')
Then biting his nail and sugaring his words sweet:
'Keep your head, Mr Dooley. Religion is clearly not up
    your street.
But let me ask you as a plain patriotic fellow
Whether you'd stand there so smug and yellow
If the foe were attacking your own dear sister.'
'I'd knock their brains out, mister,
On the floor,' I said. 'There,' he says kindly, 'I knew you
    were no pacifist.
It's your straight duty as a man to enlist.
The enemy is at the door.' You could have downed
Me with a feather. 'Where?' I gasp, looking round.
'Not this door,' he says angered. 'Don't play the clown.
But they're two thousand miles away planning to do us down.
Why, the news is full of the deeds of those murderers and
    rapers.'
'Your Eminence,' I said, 'my father told me never to
    believe the papers
But to go by my eyes,
And at two thousand miles the poor things can't tell truth
    from lies.'
His fearful spectacles glittered like the moon: 'For the last
    time what right

Has a man like you to refuse to fight?'
'More right,' I said, 'than you.
You've never murdered a man, so you don't know what it
   is I won't do.
I've done it in good hot blood, so haven't I the right to
   make bold
To declare that I shan't do it in cold?'
Then the judge rises in a great rage
And writes DOOLEY IS A TRAITOR in black upon a page
And tells me I must die.
'What, me?' says I.
'If you still won't fight.'
'Well, yes, your Honour,' I said, 'that's right.'

Alice, My Servant in Jamaica

Alice among the ducks at the garden bottom
With mucky words knows how to curse eggs
Blue and nourishing for a breakfast from them.
And higgledy-piggledy the devoted necks
Worship in gabble her wicked figure down
By the duckpond. Unlike all her sex,
She can wipe a mirror and not look at her own
Reflection, and pick up long-legged insects.

To her department of the beeswaxed floors,
Vine-drilled veranda, shining door-handles,
The daily dignified ambassadors
Through vegetable squalor upon mineral splendour
Of official bicycles ride out to surrender
In a sack the town's citadel of scandals.

At Any Rate

'He's dead,' they shouted as he left his motorbike
And catapulted twenty foot through air
And dented earth. They wanted him to be dead
Out of a sort of innocent malignance
And being born dramatists the lot of them.
And dead he was in the end. The blood gushed
From his ears, 'He's dead,' they told the doctor,
Though he wasn't, as the doctor saw at once,
By any means dead. 'Officer,' they said, 'he's dead.
He ought to be, at any rate if he's human.'
And in the end they were right, dead right.
An hour later, by the tangled bike
(Considered by the crowd by no means done for)
They were still standing, very much alive –
As they ought to be, at any rate if they're human.

Three Dreams

1

Hair long, cheekbones high,
Unencumbered by manners, though clothed in the costume
    of an age,
I meet you, have always known you, used cunning and
    knives to win you in primitive epochs and other lives,
Woman with a tinge of African or Spanish.
We give no sign of recognition, I single you out at parties,
    we face each other at crossroads, I swim round a
    headland and there you are on the beach, conscious of
    me,
Eyes wide open.
You swerve aside. I follow,
Tracking you through the old familiar wilderness,
Unhurried because there is no time, unanxious because I
    am sure to find you
Beneath the oak or catch you under the sea,
In sympathy unlike human sympathy, which is mixed with
    a grain of contempt,
With love not made a lie by the pert desire for discovery,
With love we do not need to name.

2

I see islands floating unknowingly on to the bows of foreign
    ships and sunk
(Gone the name of the archipelago),
The wading ashore, the scuffle in the shallows or the
    cliffside barrage;
The chief consults unruffled, trusting in the local science

And the latest modifications in the arrow.
His sons are soon dead. The women go to the mountain.
High above the sea-shore vegetation flies the morbid,
    multicoloured flag.
I see the Roman in Bavaria
Baffled by the fir-devils, the miles of fir, the sneering
    ravens;
The Spaniard breathing with difficulty in Peru,
Or afraid, for fear of laughter, to skate on the Dutch
    canals.
The Hawaiian turns his face away from me, dying of the
    imported germ.
Crete swarms with a new shape of head,
Makers of the prettiest daggers the Minoans are astonished,
    killed to a man.

Wandering I visit the last Carib lying in a corner, the lost
    Etruscans,
And empty of Red Indians the cheerless plains.

3

The Siberian tiger sits on a cliff of snow
Casting a blue shadow bigger than himself
And destroys with his mouth the appealing, flying deer.
I too tear the haunches and eat the strings and the guts,
The glance of the victim still upon me.
Only I know the true wickedness of the tiger.
His whiskers and eye compel me. I must scurry to please
    him.

The sunny lawn is littered with deadly snakes,
Walk as warily as you may, you are bound to wake them.
Aimed elsewhere my sole treads on the slumbering ribbon,

My shoe squelches the puff adder, the mamba strikes
    through my leggings,
All around alarm of tongues, coilings, ill colours, outrage,
    directed malice,
Till I fall on the sunny lawn, a small Laocöon.

In a gap in the forest I come upon the lion and the wolf
Fighting to the death, the lion losing,
His face gory, righteous, amazed.
He is the king. He has no right to lose.
But the wolf, who is guilty of winning, with a long clever
    look
Tears down the lion.
Hiding in a tree,
I love the wolf for this unnatural revolt.

But I am seen. Suddenly a crowd assembles,
Inflamed country faces, farmers with their sons and dogs,
Their pursuit ponderous, full of apparatus.
Running, never quite flying,
Weak I watch my webbed prints in the wet sand recede
    behind me.
I kiss the befriending trees, I confide in the river, the
    ripples are on my side,
Storming through legs, assisting speed.
Perfect my hiding-place in the reeds till each time by
    chance discovered.
From deep in the mud-bank they haul me out straining to
    use my wings,
For spying to be done to death with sticks.

Girls' School

Bound by a bell's sound, the prayer, the quarrel, the test
Cannot assume capital letters and monomaniacal
Adult faces. The perfunctory is best

For young girls, who will learn the way far too soon
To put all their eggs in one basket, all the heart in a look,
And curse specialisation under a later moon.

But now in the milky dormitories they sleep without fuss
Because it is the time for it; as happy to lie by night
Under a quilt as by day on a chequered syllabus.

The hours, pretending they do not know how to combine,
Walk up as charming freebooters, unarmed, disclaiming
Allegiance to that remote and iron-grey battle-line.

Around, the lavatories, the tennis courts and the tinny
Pianos gather initials. Vanishing in a whisper
Or on a piece of paper crumpled in the spinney,

Love is too temporary to be right or wrong.
Somewhere the staff functions, but vaguely, like a hand
Reaching over the gramophone to alter the song

Or prevent the needle sticking in a sentimental groove.
In dreamlike crocodiles they think impregnable or lonely
Perambulations or cotton crowds, listless the girls move

To their first continuous event, the stream the mists cover,
Which is waiting to call Ophelia those who will find it
A flood their love or terror can never get over.

Love, Death and the Snowstorm

Listen to the cry
Of the snow, the audible wailing of a falling sky.
Each white and individual shred
Goes moaning on the convulsive voyage of becoming dead.

The keen Chinaman at random takes
One flake, and makes
A landscape of it; out of the complicated storm of crystal
Esteems a single flake a moon, a vestal
Portent, a repose, till, touching ground,
Its commonness is found.

Love too is oriental. Love can assert
That what is common as dirt and ultimately dirt
Is a rare earth. Convincingly will tell you
The more than real is the fairest value.
And can say, whatever the juries cry,
There is no such thing as deserving to die.

Hand in Hand

Through the neat glade, a disgusting
Bird on every twig,
Two stroll defiantly trusting
That the forest is simple and big.
But eyes in the boles
Have marked them, and, suggesting urinals,
A susurrus breaks from the leaves of the fig.

They may hold like amulets
Precious hands, or go linking
Arms, but no one gets
Cleanly through without slinking.
Quite innocent,
Moving to kiss, although they hadn't meant
To, they find themselves archly winking.

On every branch a sparrow,
An eye in every bark
Shooting a heartless arrow
With initials to its mark.
Bleeding, love turns
To share the doom of the beast that learns
Africa is an amusement park.

What Day Proved the Dark Denies

Deep in bed lie the Jew-baiters.
In loving arms the peace-haters
Grab sleep like a marriage right
From the acquiescent night.
Now neither pain nor money has
Much to say. The national jazz
Dies on the short wave, uniform
Cools on the peg, and through the warm
And prone person from head to toe
Harmless electrocutions flow.
What day proved the dark denies,
Shiningly false, till the cock cries.
Then the aggressive noises come
To seize the ear and pound its drum;
Hounded from each hiding-place,
Guilty of their night's embrace,
Colours regroup, under whose flags
Sight, roughly conscripted, lags,
Dishonouring the lids' firm truce;
And the face so mild and spruce,
Trying out the soldier's deed,
At the razor starts to bleed:
Slight infection which, before
Night intervenes, could spread to war.

Closing Time

Jerusalem Street and Paradise Square
Drive their drinkers home to bed.
Dreaming of fancy houses where
The sheets are white and the lanterns red,
Drunkards grouped round the baby grand
With moonlike face and waving hand
Leave. The seedy last who lingers
Through the tankard sees his fingers.

Turned out in boastful threes and twos,
The champions at darts and soccer
Have hearts that sink into the shoes
That lead them back towards the knocker,
Kick stones, throw sticks dejectedly,
And whistle disconnectedly.
And, as they think about their wives,
The rain returns into their lives.

The Ghost of an Education

Muzzy with drink, I let my humour recline
By the river border, watching satire dip,
First as a summer streamer, next a whip
Cracked at the surface, then a fishing line
Pulling the past reluctant from its bed
In vague and tangled shapes. Odd fish, half dead
Bogies, and old disguises worn no longer
Dripped up, now honest scarecrows. Consternation
Saw last an ancient horrifying conger,
The long lie that was my education.

Assurance gone, satire began to quiver
Till it broke, and the thing hauled up fell back in the river,
Where it lives, with the price of my freedom on its head,
Scaring strangers, slowing the current, fouling the bed.

Isles of Scilly

Here the seal smooths her familiar pillows
On rock, here fin and beak,
Harming nobody,
Seek
And hide in the sea. Inland, shin-deep in the shallows,
Horses like saurians lift up their necks.

The summer isles where winter seldom hardens
The soft print of the cow;
Unforbidden,
The bough
Gratefully relaxes in the snakeless gardens,
And the wave's blue crystal tells the truth to gazers.

The postman, like a parent, gives good-day
In the morning to the stranger,
But his bright box
Is a danger
Signal. Keep the thoughts of home away!
For thoughts of home are thoughts of your escape,

And only those who need no haven are sure
To find one here. The rose,
Price calculated,
Glows
Redder to the grower than the epicure
Hoarding up scraps of sights for his return.

Daphne

From her imaginative arms
    Sometimes there has come
Such a downpouring of gesture
    That it has startled the room
Back to be a cave and made
    Virgilian images bloom

From the sad modern ground.
    No repetition but time
Can I find in her country,
    No one thing the same
In a day and a night's journey
    But her reuttered name.

NEW & SELECTED
POEMS
1983

For Dylan Thomas

Only Prose was pleased when he was dead
Who housed more music in his bulbous head
Than all the cupolas that have hummed with singers,
And wrung more chimes from his chubby fountain fingers
Than twelve bell-ringers, arms all going together;
Yet made of life such heavy-hearted weather
That neither love nor money kept him warm,
For wherever he slept or drank his pet storm
Of imagination followed him around,
Till it turned rogue and clawed him to the ground.
Unregarded now, like plain girls, are the words
He gave fine moments to, stiff as dead birds
The images he flew to altitudes
Unbreathable before, and solitudes
Again the deserts he drove his rhythms through,
Biblical and furious as Jehu,
Lonely as Rimbaud, crazy as Canute,
In obstinacy and thirst to the absolute
Joy of the last line.
            When poets die,
Good poems alone, like Loki, refuse to cry;
But the more natural world will always remember
How he toppled from that high week of November
On to his jagged rock. And still we peer
Over the edge for an echo but can hear
Only the surf, see nothing but haze.

Since nobody can pull the ropes of praise
As well as he did for Ann Jones, I've dared
To try to toll for him, finding I cared
More than I thought I could him being dead
Who doesn't care and stays all day in bed.

Proposal

For all that conjuring miles can do
With rosy gauze or a black curtain,
You still seem matter-of-fact and certain;
And, when I remember, you are you
And still not too good to be true.

But if the curving earth is set
On forcing horrible reflections
Of its own hunchback on our affections,
Then let us agree to try to forget
And meet, if again, as we first met.

Nine Times

Nine times worse than abandonment by woman,
Because unappealable, because superhuman,
Is the scorn of the Muses – and rarely the wiser the poorer
Poet. Nine times, too, cooler than Nora
Walking out of her Doll's House of sham
With a flourish of doors is the quite soundless slam
With which inspiration leaves. Back jumps the Sahara,
Bringing the long-faced grasshoppers which are a
Burden, rubbing their legs and making grimaces,
Till paper becomes the parody of an oasis,
A patch of drought in a world of jeering garden.
God knows how those divine girls can harden
Their hearts against the old devoted beaux
Who fucked so boisterously once. God knows
How poetry greys insensibly to prose.

To My Daughter

When I'm far out in drink, your musical box
Gives me the horrors. Mermaids on the rocks,
Beached rabbits, stranded starfish, teddy bears –
Simpering pyknic picnickers in pairs –
To a terrible *rallentando* tinkle pass
Across a thumb-hazed sky of plastic glass.
Then you rewind the sea-song that's run down
And paddle in glee, my darling, while I drown.

Ladies

So, what distinguishes
Ladies from women?
It's not that the others
Are what is called common,
But that ladies are rare.
They can go swimming,

For instance, naked
Without a self-glance,
They can lounge unasked
And content at a dance,
And yet move, and strike,
Like a fer-de-lance.

Ladies tell lies,
But of the best sort,
And they also tell truths
When they're truly caught,
For their credible words
Follow the heart.

When cornered a lady
Never takes cover;
What she *may* take, though,
Is a different lover
Before she's quite thrown
The last one over.

No lady, lastly,
Since the bad world began
Has blamed it on apples
Any more than
Would – if there were one –
A gentleman.

Gentlemen

It didn't have that much to do with class.
I don't believe I'm squinting through a glass
Tinted by age or alcohol, but I swear
There used to be people about who had an air
Of modesty, resolve and openness,
Who did more than they promised and said less
Than you expected – not charm-strangled cadgers,
Tweed-muffled fakes or self-promoted majors,
But soft-voiced, humorous gentlemen. The word
Looks antique, awkward. Nowadays it's heard
On the mouths of auctioneers and mostly seen
In toilets or Appointments by the Queen.
There'll always be heroes, but I miss the panache
Of the quiet man with the unfunny moustache.

Double Blind

When I was young, myopic eyes
Excused me well from seeing decay,
    And as for my demise
    So blurred was the small gap
It seemed unfigurably far away.

Near sight improves? That's not my truth.
I still can't read the big word *die*;
    Worse, don't recall the youth
    With the same handicap
Who never saw me when he waved goodbye.

Our Troops

A lorry-load of soldiers (petrol chokes
The timid evening) puts the road behind,
Red-faced and joking. Let them keep their jokes
Stuck on their faces till they come to find

Laughing unseasonable. They've laughed too much,
Their humour's gone. So, children, please don't cheer,
Don't wave at them, above all do not touch,
Or they might flare up hectically and veer

Backwards. The motive of these loyal flags,
Mindlessly boomeranging, could arrive
To decorate our town with bones and rags
And leave the light the only thing alive.

Discoverer

White and curved as a shell she lies
On the long dune of the bed,
Mother-of-pearl in her nails and eyes;
    In her head
Oceanic themes have stirred
    Through leaning
Galleries sea-meaning
    Without foam of the word.

Who found the shell still hardly breathes
Lest he derange the music. Ear
Flattened against her body's wreaths
    To hear
The pulse of pleasure seized,
    He ponders
Over her name, and wonders
    At woman pleased.

Bad Dada

Charged by the music police
With issuing false notes
The hangdog oboist
Scuttles on tropical ice

Viewed from sofas on cliffs
With raptest inattention
By a superb committee
Of Second Empire stiffs.

Unease! Absence of germs,
Metaphor, weather! But under
The lee of a limp crag
Something of interest squirms,

Ochreous, vermiform –
The sort of birth one's hands
Itch to cram back inside
The raped womb of the norm.

Alone on the Beach

I wish you were here on this long occasion.
Your patient, almost Asian
Application to pleasure
Would have passed the examination – subject: Leisure.

Sun loves the truly lazy, and despises
This fidget who compromises
Between enjoyment and regretting
No work to blight, no you to bless the setting.

Tulips

Lean spiritual hounds on long green leashes,
Violently, soundlessly,
Tulips throng in the house on their intense way somewhere
    else.
Glorious with self-regard, each hard bud bends forward
In an access of concentration
To define pellucidly, to be
Indisputably tulip –
As though, if it relaxed, anyone could make a mistake!

For a week we are the journey, interposed place,
As they run through us
Into ruin and beyond.

They ignore us,
Yet in passing seem to imply a human fault.
Lucky the room used, without acknowledgement,
For their short cut to death.

For a Divorced Friend

Kind person who pulled down
A house that stood in the way
To a rubble of habits, resume
   Your gentle nature
   And grooved day.

Two rooms are your good luck —
Needless to wish you more,
For a wish seems pompous, a flourish
   Like the tick on a sum,
   And anyway your

Right answers will all find you
In the end. So little fuss
Is sure to escape the baboon's
   Intelligence,
   His animus

And viler praise. Since you bribe
Nobody, nobody sounds
The trumpet you don't need to hear.
   You want nothing but love,
   Thousands of pounds

And music. Friends you allow,
But few manage to last,
Their disorderly topicality
   No match for the clean
   Aces of the past.

Leave the door open. May I
Remain one of them who drops
By when a record's playing
   And is noticed with pleasure
   Before it stops?

Frosty Poem

In New York City I wasn't told
That mid-May nights in Vermont can be cold.
Outside, our brook, short of sun
And wind, barely keeps up a run,
Just jogs and limps so as not to freeze;
Flexing her black tender knees,
The mare between the moon and the gate
Crops fiercely as if she couldn't wait
For the calories to turn to heating,
And is blindly warming herself by eating;
Overhead, chipmunks shiver in rows,
Or heaps, or whatever racial pose
Chipmunks adopt; if there were lights,
The woods would be circus-crammed with sights –
Hedgehogs on inchmeal expeditions,
Toads in cool conjugal positions,
Somewhere the bug that bit me lying
Jubilant with my blood and dying,
Jays, if you can imagine it, keeping
Quiet, drops from bathers creeping
Back to huddle inside the lake,
And in the corridors where the snake
Exerts his snakiness unmolested
The hiss and wriggle being rested.
Fur-blanketed, a log fire lit,
I enjoy a comfortable bit
Of fellow-feeling: I can spare
That much for anyone out there.
Indeed, as soon as the next sun breaks
Itself on the farm's edge and makes
A yolky breakfast on my wall
I'll share it gladly with you all.

Message to Geneva

Now that you've gone away
The words creep out to play
And, unafraid of being hurt
By irony however
Tender, content to be small, say
'Yes, I love you with all my heart.'

This spring morning as you wake
To wallpaper and lake
To dance in front of a puritan city
Thawing Switzerland,
I melt with it and want to make
The opposite of an epitaph to your beauty.

Counting the days (like sheep
They jam the gates of sleep),
I've worked at the vulgar sums of hope;
But tomorrow our hearts, colluding
Like a partners' winning trick, will leap
To join on the green table of Europe.

Meanwhile the room looks bare,
And from his dreamy lair
Of picture-frame the painter's lion
Surveys a bed as big
As the old California, where
Our imagination is staked by the million,

And quizzes a moody man
Who hasn't any plan
But to study clocks ticking and striking,
Read weather, and solve
As decipherably as he can
The cloud lines of your forehead, making

The terror of happiness
Dog you less and less
Till it loses the scent, and the fear of words
Cower and turn tail,
So that with any casual guess
You can baffle the sphinxes along your roads.

My mind goes running wild
Over the skyline, to a child
That might land like a picnicker on our shore.
I write this quickly down
Before we meet and my self-styled
Pride shuts its never-locked door.

Biography

Though he lacked the true vocation, undeterred
He stuck to what he had chosen – a hedonist
Who crouched all night in the park but somehow missed
     Catching a wild bird.

At first how many tame geese he misled!
With the furious ingenuity of a Zeus
Condescending to swans, he used to seduce
     Dozens in the reed-bed.

Then the trick failed him, at an earlier age
Than he expected. Now he mounts a show
Of altruism; yet if you were to blow
     Your nose clumsily he'd rage

Inwardly. That he 'cares' he has often told
Himself, and proved it by weeping at Great Art.
But the unkempt tragedies of the next-door heart
     Find him tidy and old –

Old but still much more alive than dead.
He might say, 'I have feelings that you cannot guess.'
That would make us like him even less,
     So he looks it but leaves it unsaid.

Midas

Once the cheap thrill was over –
Turning parrots to brooches, jaundicing geraniums,
Freezing, baroquely, fountains –
He doomed his friends as he met them and, clutching
    statues,
Became appalled.
Soon, in a world too valuable, he pawed
Each day to death, and then regretfully
Was again the next one's murderer and chief mourner.
By now his future
Smelt of the sultry sweetness of the past.
Even after he'd learnt not to touch,
When he mixed with his people
They moved stiffly – 'The king
Gives us a minute like a vase, but we dread
To shatter it' – and made their best excuses.

Observation

Walking to our respective graves
In superb weather,
I trailed a young duke across Green Park.
The trousers made some difference. All the same,
The conclusion to which I came
Was either rich or stark:
By the way his hands were locked together
I knew we were both slaves.

Ago

Midnight at our backs and fifteen milestones
slumped exhausted by the way,
we walked into Dorset while the moon, reeling,
glowered the colour of barley
and each star was quite distinct.
Then my friend, who was mad and given to
   understatement,
paused by nettles and a gate and
between the fall of his hair and the bowl of his fingers
struck a match.
Detonation. Hush.
As a raindrop sprints on a pane
a hare poured flat-eared along the lit meadow –
but not in fear.

Romantic Experiment

In the slovenly laboratory we call
Society sometimes a poet will crawl –
Great big unsupervised baby – up the wall
And from a bottle on the topmost shelf
Marked *Danger, Do Not Touch,* or *Self,*
Swallow, and in the slow paralysis
And death that follow scrawl
In blood, vomit or piss:
'God damn you all,
God bless you too – but don't drink this.'

Doreen

All day, apart, she bakes
Nude flesh. With what intent?
That those who make mistakes
Should fancy it was meant

For what, by God, it's not.
Sun-tanned and cold to us,
But to herself the hot
Sister of Narcissus,

All night, alone, Doreen
Muffles her sex with cloth,
Hostess to the unseen
And cunnimordant moth.

Good Morning, Good Evening

My big soft duchess with the housemaid's hands
That feather-duster from my cornered mind
A generation of dead moths and send
Butterflies blooming down my spine – hallo.

My hard oracular peasant who understands
That we can see each other best when blind
And that a silence need not have an end
And that a quarrel is a pause – hullo.

My cloud, my dromedary, who crossed the sands
With rain and rescue when I was resigned
To throat-constricting irony, best friend,
Whore, mother, sister, daughter, queen – hello.

There are three teasing and adoring greetings,
Variously spelled to signify
The vivid differences among our meetings,
Not the dead sameness when we say goodbye.

The Pacifists

Since we're insipid haters
And so hate to have a fight,
How come that overnight
We wake to such ugly craters
In our small lawn? Mole-spite?
No, *we* are the perpetrators

Of damage. When it's too hard
To communicate by signs,
We sow unwitting mines
And snoringly bombard
Our own quivering lines
While sleep is changing guard.

Yet if other, actual tanks
And guns (for which I half pray)
Were to point at us both in broad day,
We might perhaps give thanks
To have found a military way
To surrender, or close ranks.

Hopeful Lies

The lies we tell are only hopes
With kinks in them like periscopes:
When we're submerged and all at sea,
They aim at visibility
Over the choppy interval, and
With luck offer a glimpse of land.

The Last Wasp

When light dims to an early blur
    Which makes me dream I'm going blind;
When the last wasp, colourless fur,
    Blends with the carpet; when I find
Soles chilled by linoleum, the moon
    Rotten and low, and bonfire smoke
Perplexing the late afternoon
    With tears that irrigate and choke;
When mist with mortuary breath
    Doodles on windows notes for death;

When with a histrionic sigh
    The year turns its face to the wall
Of winter and pretends to die,
    Then is the time I like to call
Its bluff, and either counter-attack
    By rushing into love and work,
Or take the long, muddy slog back
    Through memory. Either way, the jerk
Of one or the other blistering rope
    Tightens and lifts some flag of hope.

RECENT POEMS
1983–93

My Mother

After a corpse you need to touch a child,
Or make one, get warm anyhow. It's mild
September, and though I light a fire and pull
A thick jersey on, through walls and wool
And letter-box and telephone the cold
Gets to the bone. She was extremely old
And died asleep in her own bed; yet still
There's affront, puzzle, unease. On a Welsh hill
A week afterwards I bask and shiver
Trying to recall a young mother I never
Told either lies or truth to, from whose side
I caught a bad dose of hilarity, pride
And myopia, so that we laughed together
But kept grief fiercely independent, whether
It was shared or not. Her nose was as sharp as a pen.
Green fields? May hers be like this one. Amen.

Good Books, Bad Times

Good books in bad times (for all loyalty ends)
Can turn their backs on you, like close friends
Who don't know half the truth, and from the shelf
Cut dead the miserable anorexic self
That's lost its appetite for words, that finds
Print inflicts snow-dazzle, and the mind's
Capsized by logic, and one paragraph
Of the funniest man on earth can't raise a laugh.
To stop loving, or being loved, is to stop
Reading, is to stop. Woodland becomes backdrop
And weather mere performance. Then books stare
Like stuffed predators with a blameless air
Of enmity.
        Men, women, you dog-eared lovers
With wine-stained pages and much drabber covers
Than when you were brightly bought, before you secede
From the old union, reread, reread.

Wedding Poem

Tie chosen, shoes shined,
   I stand by my ex,
For the day recombined,
   Ocean-severed by sex –
Calentures, typhoons, doldrums, mutinies, mermaids,
   wrecks;

For our son's knot is tied,
   Whether granny or reef,
He leans on his bride,
   And in jubilee grief
His mother hoists, flag or rag, the equivocal handkerchief.

Is the gravy train
   Off? The good ship
Launched? Or the plane
   On a foredoomed trip?
Will the car be scrapped or swapped? Will the tandem end
   in a skip?

Nothing is certain
   But hopeful hearts,
Ours, yours. The curtain
   Goes up, it starts!
Play your serio-comic-pragmatical-marital parts

Con brio, con amore,
   Dear Anna and Jake,
Construct a good story
   That stands up, and make
Children who like both you and themselves, and no
   mistake.

Enjoy long silence
  Of the right sort,
May your rare violence
  Be sweet and short,
And all your news be dull, except for gossip and sport.

For Any Correspondent

This morning's risible memorandum reads:
'Clock, cheese, coal, car, plug, thingummy, garbage, weeds'.
Wisdom, new and old gurus say, consists
In jacking the grovelling boredom of such lists
Up to the level of human interest.
All day, midnight on the clock, I've done my best
To achieve that erection. Now street lamps
Illuminate serious duties. Envelopes! Stamps!

Song

'Because I'm almost as glad
To be miserable as I am
Unhappy to be sad,'
Said the lone bird to the lamb,

'I'll attempt a song.' And the raven,
On his worst day of despair,
Cocked his beak towards heaven,
Gulped icy air

And cawed some half-choked words
Of praise. They made no sense
To the January birds –
A nest-bound audience

Who found fault with the metre
And the notes – black, false and wrong.
But the lamb and the snow looked whiter:
The point of any old song.

Xmas with Ex

Mistletoe poisonous, holly
Unconvincingly jolly,
And the Box turned on at ten. 'For Christ's sake, no
   cartoons?'
My sons groan. 'On one channel there's a load of loons
Singing olde-worlde hymns, and on the rest the same vicar
(OK, ones a bit thicker and the other slightly sicker)
Telling us to rejoice
And saying unfunny things in a funny sort of voice.'
'Anyone for a stroll?' I propose.
They give polite and individual noes.
So off I trudge
On the old routine: across the river sludge
Choked with detritus –
Tyres, bottles, condoms, prams, probably a foetus –
Till I reach the park. It looks empty and delightful,
But in its own way is equally frightful:
A few dedicated (to what or whom?) joggers,
A dozen loud, proprietorial doggers,
Plus a lone madman on the tennis-court practising serves,
   tossing a grimy ball
Over and over again and letting it fall
Unstruck. Averting my eyes
From the new statuary, low-class, high-rise,
I wish a lad Happy Christmas, but he is too shy –
Or is it too disordered? – to reply.
Only the ducks look cheerier
Than usual, reprieved from popular bread-throwing
   hysteria.
Then down the King's Road, which for once has lost its
   shabby razzmatazz
And this morning has
Nothing to show but a few queer folk and cars

Looking as if they'd just landed from Mars.
And so back home,
Where all roads lead more often than to Rome.
For me, as pagan
As Horace or Hitler or Fagin,
This Christmas
Feels oddly like a missed Mass –
Though quite what's missed, and what imaginably might
   be Mass,
And where home is, baffle, alas.

Half-light

Light byzantinely gold and flat
Flakes from an evening that seemed holy
And everlasting, but is slowly
Degenerating. I can't read;
Try to decipher. Look, the weir
Is vitrified by its own speed.
Willows and swallows double. A cat
Plays tiger, clown and acrobat
In a circus round the fuchsia bush
Burning with reinvented red.
Hinting at truths to see or hear,
Aureoled, every shape moves near,
But only to illude, recede
Into illegible night. Dusk, hush
Tease me with riddles, similes,
Hallucinations, so that unease
Outnumbers peace. Human one, please
Take me to morning through our bed.

The Aristocrats

Careless of petit-bourgeois shame,
They bent the rules yet played the game.
Now they're just people in old homes
Distinguished by a lack of gnomes.
The richer ones invest, keep zoos,
And have no favourites among Jews,
Arabs and Texans and town-planners.
The poorer sort adhere to booze,
Grandparents, grand pianos,
Bad luck, bad heating and good manners.

Last Night

Last night as I was dreaming
Badly, from nowhere you leant down
With such hilarity of love
But such anxiety of frown
That sweat-soaked, quilt-tugging carphologist,
I struggled sticky seconds to move
Across the seventy miles
To touch, to reassure you
That nothing in me can endanger your smiles
And that something in me might cure you
Of the sense of being or seeming
At fault, of lacking full right to exist.
In my next dream we kissed
And pulled a chicken-bone, and each made a wish.
Yours, like all your desires, was criss-crossed with tape
And under secret seal
(Was it for advance? retreat? escape?);
Mine, like all mine, I publish
As the shameless news of my world:
To see you happily, painfully, curled
In a strange bed,
Then opening those long legs wider than ever to reveal
A brand-new body to make you feel,
As mine used to do,
Undispossessably you
And glad for good not to be dead.

Metaphors Mixed for Two

He: Violin changes to cello. Feeling sinks deeper,
　　To lie unruffled in the dark underwater
　　Developing every sense but sight – the pitch
　　Where love need not be visible as such
　　And the word, less used, is more rarely abused. At last
　　Desire and confusion calm down to a cast
　　Of mind, a systole, a prejudice,
　　Perhaps the only gracious one there is:
　　Presumptuous, yes, and rigid, but not therefore
　　　　wrong,
　　For some prop for courage is needed on the long
　　Joint trek. . . .
She: But are you ready to explore
　　Further, to find miles of disorder more –
　　Dumb, boundless country cowering under storm,
　　Sky wishing hard, not knowing how to be warm,
　　Breaking from queer quarters rain, a deceptive curtain
　　Hiding God knows what, only deception certain,
　　Monster-filled terrain appalled to have been the cause
　　Of its loneliness? The sirens round those shores
　　Sing with domestic sweetness from the foam
　　But can make rocks their comfortable home,
　　While inland the natives are in two minds whether
　　To greet the adventurer, or die struggling together.
He: I too can be difficult. Jehovah, I tie knots
　　For the pleasure of slashing them; search for weak
　　　　spots
　　To bully or nobly forgive. . . .
She: And, running, I drop
　　Dud favours like Atalanta's apples – you stop
　　And pick them up, thinking them signs of victory,
　　While I look back, embarrassed, valedictory,
　　Longing to renounce them.

He: So what shall we do
　　If I am smug and a fool and you are . . . you?
She: Remain, or become, ourselves. Don't ask to be told,
　　Or you'll find me twice as willing – and half cold.

Is a Rose a Rose?

A pig under a tree in the Peloponnese
Is a pig under a tree . . . But add to these
Facts of zoology, botany, geography,
A south wind, fulvous evening, you and me,
Fecundity and idleness, then snap!
Memory's caught in a photographic trap,
And birth and death and marriage won't efface
That animal, one olive and the place.

Public Incident
for Edward

You looked at me with such unjustified trust –
In this case that I'd got a joke –
That I felt, in the street, my throat choke.
Then a woman gazed at you with such pure lust
To kidnap you, or any tot,
With the benevolence of the witch
Mad to boil small boys in a doting-pot,
That I moved on, with you and the joke I hadn't quite got,
Happy in my humorous half-possession.
Not that one owns much, not
That one is in any particular way rich,
Not that one knows quite how to love. Which
Is an everyday confession.

Because We'd Talked
for B.B.

Because we'd talked of suicide at length
And you died on your day of birth, there goes the tenth
Good friend, I thought, guilty of bad taste,
Not to mention (which is to brood on) waste;
But it wasn't so. You, who'd had five wives,
Five children, numberless lovers and nine lives,
Performed a gentle disappearing act,
Leaving the wraith of the grin you never lacked.
'Off with his head!' 'Don't look at me like that!'
Their Majesties screamed at the unconventional Cat,
But long before he melted into air
He'd promised Alice, 'I shall see you there.'
And so he may, or not: we atheists
Mourning each other cannot make the mists
Lift entirely. Since I don't have to rank you
With the other dear disgraceful corpses, thank you
For that, and what you knew best how to give –
As host or guest – the appetite to live.

On and Off Stage

The woman with the face
That ripples all over the place
   Transparently or slyly
Frets at the bank of the man
Of stone, who is dead-pan,
   Near-truthfully, dryly.

Both are hopelessly loyal;
But she demands the royal
   Dramatic prerogative,
And he, born actor too,
Grimly refuses to woo
   Beyond what his role can give.

When the property crockery shatters
And all, or nothing, matters
   And Medusa gibbers, 'Love me!'
A statue with shifting eyes
Deadly alive replies,
   'I do; but you don't move me.'

Simple Riddle

You were an easy rhyme once though a virgin,
Until you were violated by a golfer.

You used to drive me mad at regular intervals,
But now that happens less predictably.

To Germans you're masculine, but for most of us
Woman. I still sulk for you, still miss you

When you hide. Not like your brother: he's all there,
Promoting his day-clubs for the seasonal people,

Topless, bottomless, sexless. You
Vary the veils of private nakedness.

Bath Death-wish

Five foot eleven, twelve stone, sixty-three,
I lie in the bath and look at the apple-tree
And the apples dawdling into rubicundity

To blend with the old brick wall's well-weathered red.
Already, and all ready, I feel dead:
The tub, no longer a limp invalid's warm bed,

Is a dank coffin, my flesh wrinkled fruit
For the birds, who pretend to be irresolute
But eviscerate like pterodactyls. Absolute

For death now, voyeur, écouteur, I long
To see, hear, be their breakfast – no more wrong
Or right at last, just method, satisfaction, song.

Moods, Dooms

1

On the evening when my mother was almost dying
For the first time that I know of I caught you lying.
You'd been uncannily sympathetic. Strange
That love can so expand, contract and range
Through the whole spectrum in one monochrome day.
I said nothing at the time, but felt sad
For both, and tried to reason: I too had
Shuffled words. When it comes to small betrayals,
The female's are more striking than the male's.

2

Love said stay, but pride said go.
I stayed, and stayed too long.
It hurts both love and pride to know
Pride's right and love was wrong.

3

On April the first at twelve o'clock exactly
I learnt that the Department of Life had sacked me:
As worker, poet, parent, husband, lover,
Useful employment was evidently over.
You tell me life must be lived. Which would you rather
Be, real ghost or unreal person, Father?

4

Spare a thoughtful thought, ladies and gents,
For those who are cursed with creative temperaments
Like Thomas, Chatterton or Baudelaire
But have absolutely no talent. Spare
A thought, for when they get rid of themselves
They bequeath nothing to library shelves:
All they leave is a weak pot-pourri smell.
May they rest, though friends and families cannot, well.

To Clare

No bigger than my hand, I see a cloud
    Over your mind. I comment, you deny it;
And then because we're both of us too proud
    To talk about it – silence. By and by, it
Lours, but your thunder never speaks out loud,
    Nor will your lightning ever clarify it.
So gloom persists for days, for half a week, say:
Since we're in France I'd call the weather *fixé*.

'Stormy' barometers, when gently tapped,
    Improve to 'Variable', if not 'Set Fair',
But whether you are kissed or stroked or slapped,
    Whether I care too much or try to care
Not in the least, adapt or don't adapt,
    Low pressure remains constant. Well, that's Clare.
Although I sometimes want to throw a bomb at her,
She's still my only fair, unfair barometer.

Without you in the sitting-room, the hall,
    The kitchen, not to mention rooms more private,
There'd be no meteorology at all,
    No winds to shiver in, heat-waves to revive at,
Or snow for fun, but just a cosmic pall
    (Conclusion I've been hoping not to arrive at)
Of grey, undifferentiated mist:
The self-made climate of the solipsist.

The Old Revolutionary

Friends, allies, we made our plan: to separate.
You, much the cleverer, went off as a spy,
Swallowed a tougher shape of vowel and ate
Sheep's eyes, frogs, fruit bats, inwardly
Loathing barbarian etiquette; while I
Fired rockets, declared our position, teased the enemy.

When the front became frozen, for their warmth I hung
Over your letters. Under florid ceilings,
Wittily getting diplomats drunk, you wrung
Secrets from them, and (typical of you)
Mingled caricature with hairbreadth dealings.
Laughter welled in our throats; envious saliva too.

At Christmas, when we fraternised, they tried
To talk us round, patronising our rags,
Dissuading us from seeming suicide.
Then the day came when your ultimate stratagem
Made our hearts flap on our body-poles like flags:
You announced a masterstroke – you had married one of
    them.

Soon afterwards you sent the photograph.
The oval face's delicate pointlessness –
In their men stupidity – roused in us half
Lust at the sight of a woman, half contempt.
Your report wasn't valuable. We would have minded less
If you had succeeded some other way in your attempt.

'Theory may have misled you, for the better
Class of people live with undoubted taste
And the poor look contented,' your last letter
Ended. And when all but the mad we had to retreat,
You, as the bland mediator, were placed
As governor here. I noticed your child, foreign and neat.

So now, I suppose, you're the enemy. Hate, that sun,
Burnt out, has faded to a moon, a cold
Rage literally. Crazy to point a gun
At you or anybody else, absurd
To scuffle with the new police. I'll grow old
Pottering in the laboratory of the last word.

Dear Dead

Dear dead unheroes and unheroines
Who mangled your own selves – and I've known ten,
Hectic, vivid, amusing women and men –
What's your verdict now? Are you damned for your sins?
Some said so; others shrugged kindly; a few cried
For a dislocated day or month or two
And scratched the scab of no-guilt, as friends do
(As I did) who are abashed by suicide.
But now that an old colleague of sixty-five
Has blown his brains out, I'm inclined to call
A halt to pity for self-pity. All
Those guns, ropes, razors, ovens . . . why not contrive
    Some evanescent exit, in a style
    That would raise at least the ghost of a half-smile?

Two Words

A hot, close night. From the flat above, a huge, slow sigh
From the old widower there; then, long-drawn-out, 'Oh
   dear!'
Dear who, for him? Dear grief? Dear Somebodaddy? I
Held my dear hot and close that night, in winter fear.

EPIGRAMS
and
ODDITIES

Any Man to Every Woman at Some Time

My dear, I've been doing some thinking.
The outcome is – I'm not joking –
I've decided to die, not drinking,
But working and fucking and smoking.
And now I'm going to get stinking.

The Baboon's Prayer

I chased a female up a tree
    (She had a vivid bum)
And there we raised a familee.
    O jolly axeman, come –
For we're by now too high and dry
    Inside our little hut –
And do what neither she nor I
    Can bring ourselves to: cut.

The Porter's Vision

Pushing my trolley across Waterloo,
I met another fellow. 'Who are you?'
I asked him friendly-like because his face
Seemed somehow or other rather out of place
In that great jostling terminus. His tones
Were soft. He said, 'I mend the telephones.'
Wondering, I questioned him how that could be,
For his garb was not what the Postal Company
Are wont to wear, but more a sort of sheet.
He smiled and spoke in accents passing sweet:
'I mend the lines that hum between the hearts
Of men. Transfixed by legion bitter darts,
Upon the Cross two thousand years ago
I died.' The visitant was gone – and lo,
I found my grimy cap was in my hands,
Brimming with gold as countless as far sands.

Family

The family is the ballast without which
A man might rise – into the nearest ditch.

Three Prongs

Men want women, women children, children parents:
There's a trilemma that strains all adherence.

For Bonny Elspeth

I canna thole thae fleechin folk
   Wha ca' a lassie 'goddess'
When a' their meanin is to poke
   Their neb inside her bodice.
They're unco free wi' terms like 'Muse',
   'Parnassus', 'wreaths o' myrtle' –
Ay, but the mount they hae in view's
   Her ain aneath a kirtle!

Wi' sic, an they be gi'en their boon,
   The compliments they've paid ye
Are dangit aff-hand like auld shoon
   An' barefit gaes the lady.
Sic phraisin flatt'ries I abhor
   An' leave to ither gentry;
I'd sooner be tongue-dry afore,
   An', after, complimentary.

I grant fu' readily, I feel
   The influence o' your beauty –
Indeed t'wad turn a saint a de'il,
   Ev'n juvenate Auld Clootie;
But tho' I hae the art to please
   Wi' words as weel as onie,
I wadna at ane straik, like bees,
   Surrender a' my honey.

Syne poets, let them clink sae sweet,
   Maun jangle starv'd o' kissin,
Syne ainlie angels can complete
   Their luve wi' ane part missin,
Syne fainness follows flesh an' bluid
   By Nature's dear designin –
Let's mak the inclination guid
   By hazard o' combinin!

Out of a Hot Lapis Lazuli Sky
by Pia Holst

PILOT HAS CRASHED, HITS PALO ALTO.
SHIP TAIL HOPS MILE, DIGS STREETWIDE PIT.
SHOAL OF DEAD BODIES! headline screamed.
I, Osip, survived. Condemned to phials
Of Pathosil and to palish tea,
Hot pails of it (pah, lots!) – I take
A loth sip, it's like opal shit,
Pith also (if I may lisp oath).
I'm in ward I, St Olaph's Clinic,
Potash, L.I. Being spoilt? Ah, no.
Dr Philotas lit a posh
Cigar and growled, 'Your femur's split.
Oh, a bad case. You've lost a hip.'
I spot Hal, his assistant. 'Pish,
A lot you know, Plato!' (his first name).
'Tho' a lip's gashed, I shall mend,' I said.
'Sh! Ailpot!' Doc barked. 'Hop it, Sal!'
(A pi sloth, a hot slip of a nurse,
To Phil, as to his pal, a slave).
'Pat his 'ol back, slap it. Ho! Cough please.
Phlegm like Po silt–ha! ha! Op. list?
Ta. Polish the knife, soap hilt and spit.
Hola! We lop this.' A leg goes–mine.
His plot a fact at last, I hop,
A lame, halt Osip; so Lapith did
Hamstrung by Centaur's fierce lap-hoist.
I ask you, is P.T. a hol
In hospital? Ah, pistol, end me!
Lo, ashpit yawns! Hail, post-existence!
A dark one? It may hap so, 'til
God's halo tips my soil-path trudged.

109

P.S. A litho, 'Th'oil Spa'
By Hals, I opt to leave to my holist
Pa, T.A. Hislop. Ha, I'l stop.

Notes

There are 59 anagrams of *hospital*.

Ship: = *plane*, as often.

Pathosil: A drug to relieve suffering (*pathos*), unknown, alas, to modern medicine and me.

Pith: The oath, or crude word, is of course *piss*.

St. Olaph: Correctly spelt *Olaf*. But surely the name can be *Olaph* in some language? cf. *Adolf* and *Adolph*.

Potash: Concussed, Osip makes a mistake. The town of Potash is in fact in Louisiana.

Ailpot: Valetudinarian. Cf. *fusspot*.

Op.: Operation.

Spit: For luck.

Hola!: The Greek doctor was doubtless trained at the Sorbonne.

P.T.: Physical training; therapeutic exercises for the disabled.

Post-existence: In the dictionary. The hyphen, though, is a pity.

God's halo &c.: The meaning is 'rewards my earth-journey completed.' Very Browningesque.

Th'Oil Spa: It is assumed that in seventeenth-century Holland natural oil springs were resorted to for health purposes.

Holist: A follower of holism, the philosophy of General Smuts.

I'l stop: Shavian spelling?

Huggery-muggery

Huggery-muggery
Saxo Grammaticus
As a historian
Hadn't much flair;
One might have said he was
Supererogatory
Had he not mentioned the
Hamlet Affair.

TRANSLATIONS

Carmen
Théophile Gautier

Carmen is thin; a stroke of bistre
Rings her eyes, gipsy and bandit;
Her hair has a sinister black lustre;
As for her skin, the Devil tanned it.

Women declare that she is plain,
But men all passionately adore her:
And a great archbishop of Spain
Sings the Mass on his knees before her;

For a huge coil of tawny amber
Curls and writhes over her nape,
Which let loose in the bed-chamber
Makes a robe for her sweet shape.

And out of that pallor a mouth parts
With a conqueror's laugh, pimento-red,
Geranium-scarlet, dyed by hearts
That sacrificially have bled.

Her swarthy Moorish looks defeat
More classic beauties, and the fire
That glows from her eyes' intense heat
Arouses and exhausts desire.

Her piquant ugliness has the tang
Of a grain of salt from the sour sea
Out of which cruel Venus sprang,
Challenging in her nudity.

To a Pink Dress
Théophile Gautier

When you wear that dress I am charmed,
It undresses you so well –
Makes you paganly bare-armed
And your globed breasts jut and swell.

Light as a bee's wing, fresh
As the heart of a tea-rose, the dress
Hovers about your flesh,
A pale ruby caress.

The skin to the silk lends
Shivery silver glints,
And the silk to the skin sends
Back ruddy reflected tints.

From where does this strange robe spring
Which seems as if it were made
Out of you, like a live thing
Mingling flesh with its brilliant shade?

Are those new-found colours drawn
From Venus's shell? Does that hue
Owe its pink to the dawn,
Or the nipple half bursting through?

Or is the silk, rather, dyed
By the blush of your modesty? No:
Your body is conscious of pride
From renown in the studio.

Your veil lies heavy. Uncover –
And, art's dream realised, hewed,
You would model for Canova
Like Pauline Borghese, nude.

Each rosy fold of that dress is
My mouth unsatisfied,
And the lips form a tissue of kisses
For the body I'm now denied.

The Garret
Théophile Gautier

Up on the tiles, where the cat's talons
Stalking the drinking bird risk balance,
Between two drainpipes I can see
A garret from my balcony.

Supposing that I were to lie
Like an author, I could prettify
The picture and put in, to please,
A window-box full of sweet peas,

And show you Rigolette, whose specked
And scratched small mirror can reflect
With its quicksilver only half
Of her black eyes and preening laugh;

Or Margot, dress still not yet pinned,
Bosom and hair bare to the wind,
With a water-jug creating showers
For her garden – one big pot of flowers;

Or else some young poet who curses,
Trying to scan his delphic verses,
And sees, silhouetted, each windmill
And roof of Montmartre from his sill.

But *my* garret is real, alas.
The window with its blind filmed glass
Slopes under green and rotting timber.
Here no convolvulus will clamber.

For a kept girl or an artist or
A widower or a bachelor
A loft is always melancholy.
Only in songs are garrets jolly.

In the old days, where the cramped roof bent
Two foreheads for a kiss, content
With a camp-bed love used to creep
Up to Suzon, to chat and sleep;

But now we want our joy cocooned
And pampered, must have beds festooned
By Monbro, quilted walls, the place
Awash with silk, flooded with lace.

Margot, who didn't return one night,
Stays on at the house with the red light,
And, a rich man's mistress, Rigolette
No longer waters her mignonette.

It's a long time since the poet, tired
Of catching flying rhymes, was hired
As a *journalist* and left his poor
Patch of sky for the first floor;

And through that pane one sees a crone
With a pinched profile, all alone,
Tugging interminably at
A bit of thread, scolding her cat.

The Fireside
Théophile Gautier

The deluging rain streams along roofs and gutters;
The elm by the road sways and creaks and totters
At the will of the swirling wind as it takes the shock;
From the glacier's height the ruining avalanche falls;
The torrent bays under the gorge's walls,
Mud-brown and churning huge lumps of rock.

It's freezing! What a din the relentless hail
Makes with its ricochets as it whips the frail
Pane! The north wind tires itself in despair.
What matter? Haven't I a hearth bright with flames,
A cat on my knees that invents its own games,
A book for awake, and for sleep an armchair?

Art
Théophile Gautier

Yes, beauty blooms from the curse
Of a tough form that resists
Even perfectionists –
Marble, enamel, onyx, verse.

No cramped posturing – true.
But to walk properly on-
Stage, Muse, you must don
A tight, narrow, classical shoe.

Too easy, over-worn
Rhythms that any foot
Like an old slipper can put
Cosily on or off, I scorn.

Sculptor, reject clay
Which kneading thumbs will find
Too slippery when the mind
Is absent, drifting far away;

With the guardians of the pure
Outline, with Carrara
Or Paros, harder, rarer,
Struggle – the marbles that endure;

Borrow from Syracuse
Its bronze, which will reveal
Unmistakably the appeal
And arrogance of the stroke you choose;

Or, delicate-handed, follow
And work an agate's vein
Till from it you attain
A perfect profile of Apollo.

Painter, avoid the blur
Of water-colours, and fix
The too frail tints you mix
In the kiln of the enameller;

Create out of the sea
Azure sirens who swish
Tails multiform as fish,
Prodigies blazoned in heraldry;

Paint Mary in a blue robe
With her Child, aureoled
In a triple frame of gold,
And, with the Cross above it, the globe.

Everything moves towards dust.
Only great art has strength
To match eternity's length:
The city is outlived by the bust;

And the austere medallion
Which some peasant has found
By digging up his ground
Shows a Domitian or a Julian.

The gods themselves pass.
Yet poetry that reigns
Unchallengeably remains
More indestructible than brass.

Carve with the chisel, knock
With the hammer, push the file
Until your volatile
Dream lies sealed in the obstinate block!

Landscape
Théophile Gautier

Not a leaf stirs on a limb,
Not one bird sings;
On the red horizon's rim
Twilight's flickerings;

On this side, sparse, small
Bushes, furrows half drowned,
Greyish sections of wall,
Gnarled willows bowed to the ground;

On the other, a field that ends
With a broad, water-logged ditch,
A slow old woman who bends
Heavy-loaded; beyond which

The track, which takes a dip
Into blue hills' inclines,
And unreels, like a long strip
Of ribbon, in loops and twines.

The Pregnant Girl
Anon (12th century), from the Latin

All along I had kept
My love dark, and stepped
  Carefully. Now I'm in tears,

For my secret plainly shows:
My womb has grown, and grows,
  And the child's birth nears.

Mother scolds me all day,
Father keeps out of my way,
  Two grim, unfriendly faces.

I sit in the house on my own
And daren't go out alone
  To enjoy public places.

If I do venture outside,
I'm curiously eyed
  As though I were a freak.

At the sight of this belly, men
Nudge one another, and when
  I walk past don't speak.

Below Zero
Bartolo Cattafi

In November the mercury fell,
We went below zero. The river was full
Of jaundiced plane leaves and colours that make
The eye suffer – tints
Of steel, of bitumen, of the snake
That winds through poisonous dreams.
In the cabin of our boat long since
Sunk (the first floor of a hotel
In the rue de Tours) we put on our heaviest wool
Sweaters, which moths had chewed.
The only way to pretend we were alive
Was to strike a breast, an attitude:
Then pull
The rusted chain of the emergency bell.

History
Bartolo Cattafi

Where is ancient Hellas now
With drachmas resounding like Homer's ocean?
I know nothing about that,
I have a round, flat
Telephone token, I move
Forward when the coloured signals allow
Pedestrian motion,
I beat hunger, the price of flowers is high,
Flowers which only women and corpses love,

But on my sweat-damp palm some word
Is crudely cut. Perhaps I have a soul
Able to fly
Higher than a telegraph pole,
Like the sparrow, that ordinary bird.